GOD'S BEEN THINKING ABOUT YOU!

Apostle Rodney E. Johnson

ISBN 979-8-88862-914-7

Copyright 2022 © Leeds Press Corp.
Cover copyright 2022 © Leeds Press Corp
Cover Design by Leeds Graphics.
Written by Rodney E. Johnson.
Edited by Leeds Press Corp, Staff.

Leedspublishing.com
Twitter.com/leedspresscorp
Instagram.com/leedspresscorp
Facebook.com/leedspresscorp
LP Books is an imprint of LEEDS PRESS CORP. Name and Logo trademark of LEEDS PRESS CORP. The publisher is not responsible for websites (or their content) that the publisher does not own. LEEDS PRESS SPEAKERS' AGENCY provides a wide range of authors for speaking events.
To find out more; info@leedspress.com or call 323-230- 0062
Printed in the United States of America.

TABLE OF CONTENTS

DEDICATION

This book is dedicated to believers that are walking through tough times. Know this...God's intent is always to do you good.

"For I know the thoughts that I think toward you, says the LORD, thoughts of peace and not of evil, to give you a future and a hope."
Jeremiah 29:11 (NKJV)

MY WALK WITH THE LORD

I wrote this book, God is Thinking About You, because we live in a culture that emphasizes victory and success, always being on top... but not knowing how to deal with the valleys in our lives. We must be aware that in this life, you never just leap from one mountain top to the next. Between the mountaintops, there are valleys, and in those valleys, there can be loneliness, physical and mental pains, suffering, rejection, and some of us in the valleys are forced to walk a journey of darkness not knowing where we are headed. Still, God assures us that in the midst of the valleys, He's right there with us. There was a man by the name of Watchman Née, a minister of the Gospel who passed away in a prison in China in 1972 stated, "You don't learn about God on the mountaintops, you learn about God in the valleys; it is in the valleys that we are shaped and formed." In those difficult times, God's eyes and heart constantly lead us, and we must trust Him to lead us through the valley back to the top of the mountain. After all, in each step He takes us, He is molding us to be more like him.

I was born in Sacramento, California, and was reared in a Christian home by godly parents. I had four brothers and two sisters who were all raised in the church. My father was a Baptist pastor, and my mother was an accomplished pianist excelled not only in gospel music but classical music as well. My father being not only a preacher but also a singer and my mother a pianist, it's not a wonder that we also inherited musical abilities. Singing was our trademark. We sang in church for years, all through our youth and was very involved the work that goes on in a church. This is what we did as a family. But as time went on, I came to find out that just because you are involved in church work does not mean you have a personal relationship with Jesus Christ. As a teenager, my life began to spiral in a direction that I really did not want it to go. Not understanding that the absence of my father, who passed away when I was nine years old, had a tremendous impact on my life. I know that there are exceptions when young people grow up and be very successful in life without a father, but you cannot deny the impact it has on some families who grow up in a household without the male presence. There is so much that is missed. But my mother, oh my mother, who was a praying woman was there for us through it all. I remember so many times as I would make my way to her bedroom to give her a kiss goodnight, I would find her on her knees in prayer beside her bed. Those images I will never forget because I'm sure that the prayers she prayed was for us, her hard-headed rebellious children. I do believe with all my heart that my siblings and I are what we are today because of the prayers that went up to God on our behalf.

As I mentioned before, just being involved in church work doesn't mean you have a personal relationship with Jesus Christ. As my life continued to spiral downward, I found myself getting involved in drugs. So much so, that I would be sure to carry drugs with me to church because church became very boring to me. So, in order to entertain myself, when the time was right, I would lift my finger as we did traditionally back in the day and excused myself from the sanctuary to go into the fellowship hall and indulge. After partaking, I'd come back in the sanctuary, sit in the choir stand and 'trip out' for the rest of the service. Underneath the false mask that I had developed with the drugs was a young 17-year-old young man who was extremely unhappy and miserable. But little did I know that the prayers of my mother were about to be answered in a very powerful way that would change my life forever.

I'll never forget in the month of August 1971; my next-door neighbor invited me to her church's bible study. I went, and it was very different. It was a Pentecostal setting and I recognized there was something different that I did not see in a traditional church setting. I couldn't clearly understand or articulate it at the time, but it was just something there that really got my attention. Whatever that "something" was, stayed with me and I could not shake the feeling. Even though I had experienced something different at Bible study, I was still indulging in drugs and doing things that I should not have been doing. A few weeks later, I remember going to a gospel musical. There was a song that was written that got my attention. I only remember a certain part of the song which was, "I don't want to do wrong, but I can't help myself, Lord please help me." It was the Holy Spirit that took the lyrics of that song and just impressed upon me that whole evening. I couldn't get that part of the song out of my head. It stayed with me all the way home, even when I retired to bed. I could not sleep. I tossed and turned for a long time until I had to come face to face with these lyrics. As I laid on my back, looking up through my bedroom window the words just became so strong that I had to do something about it. There I laid and began to sing with a whisper those words that were seemingly tormenting me, "*I don't want to do wrong, but I can't help myself. Lord, please help me.*" I kept singing it over and over again. The more I sang it the more my emotions were affected to the point of heart felt tears. It was about 10:00 pm and I began to feel the presence of the Lord. As I began to close my eyes, I saw the image of Christ with his arms open coming toward me and I began to weep. On the following week I was invited again by my next-door neighbor to a revival service. As I sat there as the word of God was being preached. When the invitation was given to follow Christ, I just felt compelled in a loving way to come to the altar. When I did, I was so broken inside. I couldn't hide any longer behind the mask. As I came with tears in my eyes, again I saw the image of Jesus Christ coming towards me with his arms outstretched. I was standing there weeping and then something marvelous happened. As soon as the pastor reached out and hugged me, so did the image of Jesus. I melted in his arms. His love was so strong that I could not resist it any longer. I was engulfed in his love. He assured me that He was with me and that He loved me in spite of the many things I went through personally growing up in a large family. I was 17 years old when I had that experience, I am now 68, and that experience is just as fresh as if it happened yesterday. I've been walking all these years with the Lord and I'm learning more and more about the love of Jesus. I realized you really don't know Him until you've walked through situations in your life.

"We all have a purpose in life, and when you find yours you will recognize it."-
Catherine Pulsifer

Being 17 years old, I had one more year before graduating from high school and I did not know what I wanted to do with my life. It seemed like nothing piqued my interest. I just simply did not know what to do after graduation but the usual...*go to college*. I felt much pressure from people but going to college was not in my heart to do. Nevertheless, I enrolled in college anyway and was very miserable. I just felt like there was another direction I had to take, and college was not it. My life took a drastic turn and I decided to follow my heart. I left the Baptist church and attended a non-denomination church where I began to sense my purpose in life. It is a blessing when you finally figure out what you were put here for, and I realized that I was to preach the Gospel, so I felt led to drop out of college. Dropping out of college really was a step of faith, but I knew what my heart was telling me. It was also a challenge because my mother wanted me to remain in school, which I understood completely, but the pull of God was much stronger, and I had to obey him. Being a member of this congregation, I began to learn what it was to walk with God. A lot of foundation was laid in my life in which I am so thankful.

Being within that ministry, I began to travel across the country ministering. I was with that ministry from 1972-1976. In 1976 the Lord led me to travel with another ministry. I was with this ministry from 1976-1999. We traveled and did most of our work on the Native American Reservations. We ministered mostly to the Apaches, Navajos and Crow reservations, mainly under tents, brush harbors and church buildings that were not like most of our churches. It was so rewarding. Sometimes we would spend the entire summer going from one reservation to the next. To see how hungry, they were for the Gospel taught me so much. The Lord began to teach me how much he loved them. To tell you the truth, I witnessed more conversions and miracles in the churches we went to than in the major cities. It was a learning experience to see their way of life, what they had and what life had dealt them, yet, they loved the Lord and gave their all and still do today. At that time, many did not have running water...they had out-houses...the ground was their floors, and some lived in one room homes. Yet they would travel four hours one way just to hear the gospel. Not only in the summer but in the middle of winter under blankets in the back of pick-up-trucks.

I learned that you didn't have to be technical; you didn't have to be deep; you didn't have to be eloquent. I learned that the gospel should be preached with simplicity. To this day, they still remember us, and many have gone on to be Evangelists, Pastor's, and Bishops. Only the Lord knows how many lives were affected by the gospel during those years. In 1986, we decided to start a church in Dallas, Texas. We were still visiting the reservations and other churches across the country. But during that time the Lord began to deal with me about pastoring. I did not want to pastor; I knew what pastors went through and experienced. I was happy just serving. I wasn't looking to be in the spotlight. I was just happy to serve and be behind the scenes. I was content to do whatever needed to be done so the work of the Kingdom would continue to go forward. That was my heart. So, when the Lord started dealing with me about pastoring, I fought it. In fact, I fought it for a few years. Eventually things where to the point that I knew I had to take a step of faith. I had to accept the call and so I started pastoring in 1999 in an apartment. Some time passed and was blessed with a building. I had a small congregation, and we did all we could do to grow the church, sought the Lord, and got involved in the community to do what needed to be done

We transitioned to another building, and it was at this point that Lord lead us to our covering, our overseer, who helped us tremendously. One day our Bishop called and asked if I would consider merging our congregations. I prayed about it and thought why not since he was my spiritual father, and it would be an honor to work with him. I discussed my intention with my leaders, and we were all in agreement to merge the two ministries. The merge was very successful until the enemy came in and disrupted everything. This attack was a warfare that I had never experienced. Shortly within the merge, our bishop was no longer with us. I was determined to help keep the ministry going forward. However, in the midst of doing so, I ran into roadblocks, which were horrendous. The roadblocks, obstacles and the overall spiritual warfare became more than I could bear at the time. I could no longer do what God called me to do so I resigned.

Over a period of time, I decided to pastor again and rebuild. It was the year 2007. During this season, I was working to make ends meet at home as well as in the church. It was a rough time, but the Lord saw us through it. As I look back, the Lord had me at this time teaching me many things. During this time, I had to really ponder and meditate on the things of God. It was as though the Lord had turned me upside down and began to shake previous things out of me especially previous teachings I had received. I began to realize that many things that were taught were not working for me. I knew something was wrong. I just could not bring it to a manner and way to articulate it. I did not realize how in depth it was inside me. So much of what I was hearing and witnessing within the church at this point in my life was not panning out. Something was wrong and I knew it deep within. I begin to discover that many things that were being taught was not of truth because it just wasn't working. I'm not saying that everything that was taught was wrong, but overall, for me, it just wasn't bearing witness. So, I sought the Lord in much prayer to understand what I was experiencing. Thank God for the Holy Spirit for He is the Spirit of Truth. The Lord was changing my mindset, changing my heart, changing my view of who He was according to the scriptures. I received all He was doing and working within me, and the time came when the Lord led me to leave my job to return back to ministry full time. Little did I know that He would start dealing with me about the function of an Apostle. Again, I did not want this because I understood the weight of this calling and there were many calling themselves Apostles just to have a title. I was not interested! Yet again I had to submit to Him which was His purpose for me. In my obedience, He immediately began to deal with me about the Kingdom.

I was reading the scriptures in the gospel of St. Matthew in chapter 6 when Jesus was instructing us the manner we should pray. As I began to read verse 13, *"For yours is the kingdom and the power and the glory forever,"* I believe the Holy Spirit began to allow me to see the relationship between the words, 'Kingdom Power and Glory,' an 'Expression of Manifestation.' Kingdom order is the foundation for power and glory. Without Kingdom order there will be no manifestation of power or glory. When Kingdom order is in place, not only in our churches but in our individual lives, then the power, the manifestation of God's presence is released because the order is set and when the power is released, the glory of love is revealed.

This was so important that the Lord changed the vision of our church family. He changed the name of our church from "Triune Dimensions" to "Church 1:10."

(1 Corinthian 1:10) - NABRE

"I urge you, brothers, in the name of our Lord Jesus Christ, that all of you agree in what you say, and that there be no divisions among you, but that you be united in the same mind and in the same purpose."

The name of our church, "CHURCH 1:10," is based on this scripture verse.

We understand that the vision he has given us has to do with "Intergénérational Engagement." Each generation has something to offer to the Kingdom of

God, for each generation "kisses" each other in Jesus and we work together; "Connecting People. Uniting Families. Following Christ.

My son after graduating from college with his master's degree in motion graphics, the Lord placed it on his heart to return home and work with the church. God's timing is impeccable! My son worked by bringing his expertise, along with his wife who works in education and my daughter who works in marketing/community engagement, to revamp the church's social media pages, website, and app. We are operating on a different level now; much different than the way we were before and loving it. When you find out the purpose God has for you, nothing can take its place. It is so fulfilling and satisfying. Finding God's purpose for your life is not always easy. There are many things you walk through just to prepare you for what he has for you. The late Rev. Daryl Coley sang this song, "He's preparing me for something that I can't handle right now..." God will take you on a journey that will seem so strange having twist and turns but you must learn to trust him, even when He takes you through those valleys in which we all go through. David said, "Even though I walk through the valley of the shadow of death, I will fear no evil, for you are with me; your rod and your staff they comfort me" (Psalms 23:4). Notice what he said, "Even though I walk THROUGH THE VALLEY... you are going THROUGH; not parked in it. The valley is the "Process of God" to bring you to the mountain top. Go through the valley until you get to the point when he prepares a table before you in the presence of your enemies.

God is thinking about or shall I say, God is ALWAYS thinking about you. His thoughts about you are continuous, and they are always designed for your good. When God has a purpose for you, it takes TIME for it to come to maturity. "*I know the plans I have for you, declares the Lord, PLANS FOR WELFARE AND NOT FOR EVIL, to give you a FUTURE and a HOPE.* (Jeremiah 29:11) ESV

"Wait for the Lord and be strong, and let your heart take courage; wait for the Lord." **(Psalms 27:) ESV**
God is thinking about you!

PREFACE

"God's been thinking about you." What an amazing thought! Just the idea of it places one in an inescapable frame of mind. The reality of such a magnificent thought brings you right into a personal encounter with God, a face-to-face experience that you will never forget. Knowing that God, the creator of all things, is thinking about you will not allow you to ignore the fact that you have been created for a specific purpose... a purpose that is not your own, but a purpose that is much higher than you could ever imagine.

One of the most enjoyable experiences I have ever had was to walk alongside the ocean. However simple as it may seem, in my opinion, there is nothing more breathtaking than taking the time to observe and behold the beach on a beautiful sunny day. The feeling of the cool breeze on your face, allowing your feet to sink into the squishy sand, and listening to the peaceful roar of the waves coming in and out of the shore, is a very relaxing experience. Looking out as far as the eye can see, the beauty and majesty of it all is breathtaking, and there is nothing like it. Most people take this time as a time of reflection, a time to think about their situations or about life in general. I remember walking along the beach and bending over to scoop up a hand full of sand, spreading the individual grains in the palm of my hand, and noticing the intricacy of each one. I wondered how many grains of sand I **might** have in my hand. They were so tiny, looking closely at their differences in shape, size, and color.

I compare God's creation of man to the grains of sand. Just like these grains, we have all been distinctly and uniquely made. Just as God took the time to form each grain of sand that makes up the beach itself, where there are no two grains formed alike, He also took the time to carefully create and form you differently from all others. There is a specific "detailed plan for your life" that no one can fulfill but you, for you are uniquely made and you've been singled out by God. There was no one like you before you arrived. There is no one like you now, and there will be no one created like you after you have passed. How wonderful is that?

God is truly awesome and everything that we see gives witness to He is. You were born into this world with the witness within yourself that God exists. Looking at your surroundings, there is consistent evidence that bears witness of His being. There are approximately six billion people on earth at this time, and this witness is in every one of us. Whether we acknowledge it or ignore it, we will not be able to get away from it. Everyone knows deep down inside of themselves that God exist.

In Romans, the first chapter explains this. Unfortunately, man has turned away from the witness that God put in them, and I might add...YOU have also turned away from Him. For all have sinned and come short of the glory of God. No one escapes that verdict.

God is willing and more than willing to interact with you as you continue to read this book. In fact, it is not by accident or chance that you have this book in hand now. God does all things well and complete. As Dr. RC Sproul once said, ***"There is no such thing as chance for chance is nothing, "No Thing" because chance does not exist..."*** So, you see, there is a divine plan unfolding before you. Though you may not be able to understand it now, believe me, it's real. As you read this book, I believe Grace will flow to you, enabling you to see from the heart the one you are truly encountering. Seeing God is being changed by Him, and how amazing He is to behold. To have this audience with the Master is a wonderful experience for you. Enjoy Him, enjoy who He is, enjoy His presence, and this intimate time with your Creator.

I pray that your life will no longer be the same as you encounter Him, for... God's Been Thinking About You!

CHAPTER 1

The Awesomeness of Who He Is

Awesome

(definition): *An overwhelming feeling of reverence and admiration. Extremely impressive. Astonishing, Breathtaking, Magnificent, Wonderful, Majestic Amazing.*

Is there anyone that you know that can be compared to the standard of this word? We use this word so freely without really understanding what we are expressing. We associate this word mostly with singers, writers, actors, dancers, athletes, teachers, and speakers. We have associated this word awesome when it comes to mothers, fathers, sons and daughters, policemen, lawyers, and doctors. We have practically used this word to express how we feel about many things in life. Rightly so, men and women have accomplished great things in the past and will continue to do so, but there is no one that can rightly and fully meet the true standard of this word but God. He is the Almighty, the creator of Heaven and Earth. He is absolutely incredible, indescribable, yet approachable. In the song, *"Indescribable"* written by Chris Tomlin, I believe he expresses this well...

GOD'S BEEN THINKING ABOUT YOU!

From the highest of heights to the depths of the
sea
Creation revealing Your majesty
From the colors of fall to the fragrance of spring
Every creature unique in the song that it sings
All exclaiming
Indescribable, uncontainable,
You placed the stars in the sky and You know
them by name.
You are amazing God
All powerful, untamable,
Awestruck we fall to our knees as we humbly
proclaim
You are amazing God
Who has told every lightning bolt where it should
go
Or seen heavenly storehouses laden with snow
Who imagined the sun and gives source to its light
Yet conceals it to bring us the coolness of night
None can fathom
Indescribable, uncontainable,
You placed the stars in the sky and You know
them by name
You are amazing God
All powerful, untamable,
You see the depths of my heart and you love me
the same
You are amazing God.

Why do we say He's Awesome? By what do we contribute His Awesomeness to? "HIMSELF" because He's in a class all by himself. He is who He is and who He says He is. As He said to Moses in Exodus 3:14:

"And God said unto Moses, "I AM THAT I AM."

I AM THAT I AM is not His name. He was expressing to Moses His "BEING." Moses was asking God his name for the sake of his people, but God wanted Moses to know who he was, His being. Then He told him his name. Exodus 3:15 says, *"Then God also said to Moses, "This is what you shall say to the Israelites, 'THE LORD, the God of your fathers, the God of Abraham, the God of Isaac, and the God of Jacob, has sent me to you.' This is My Name forever, and this is My name to all generations."*

I AM means that God is the only true God. I AM is the God who has always been and always will be. There is no other God besides I AM, for GOD ABSOLUTELY IS. God's absolute being means He never had a beginning, and He will never have an end. This staggers our minds. Nobody created Him. Nobody called him into being. No one sustains Him. There never was a time that He was not... and there will never be a time when He will cease to be. He simply IS and always WAS and forever SHALL BE!

If he had not come into being He could not go out of being, because He is being. He is what IS. There is no place to go outside of Him. IN THE BEGINNING, "GOD." Before one single angel was ever created, before one star was ever hung in space and named amid the billions of galaxies, before the universe itself was sustained by the word of His power, or before there was space or time, GOD IS. There is no reality before him. There is no reality outside of him unless He wills it and makes it. He is simply there as absolute reality. He is totally free to exercise authority without interference, having no restrictions. He is utterly independent; he depends on nothing to support him, counsel him, or make him what he is.

Is there anyone around who can explain God? Is anyone smart enough to tell him what to do? Is there anyone who has done him such a huge favor that God has to ask his advice? (Romans 11:34 – 35 MSG) That is what the word "absolute being" means. He is constant. He is the same yesterday, today, and forever. He is not becoming anything. He is who he is. There is no development in God, no progress for "Absolute Perfection". He cannot be Improved. God is who he is. This is the most basic fact. Nothing is more basic, and nothing is more ultimate than the fact that God is. Nothing is more foundational to the world or the universe, or your life and your future than God is. God saying to Moses, "I AM WHO I AM" is making a connection or building a bridge between his being and his name. When God said to Moses, "Tell them that I AM has sent you," he simply puts the statement of his being in the place of his name. I AM has sent me to you. The one who is... who absolutely is... sent me to you. In other words, God is telling Moses, "Before I tell you my name, I want you to get who I AM, get my being." Moses spent the first 40 years of his life in Egypt being raised in the palace, where he was educated by the finest instructors. No doubt, he was also educated regarding the many gods of Egypt.

There were, as I researched, approximately 114 gods with their main god, Amun, the king of the gods. Isis, the queen of the gods; Ra, the sun god; Horus, the king of the gods on Earth, and Anubis, the god of embalming.

I believe God was telling Moses that before you get so concerned about what my name is, where I line up among the gods of Egypt, know this, "I AM THAT I AM." I ABSOLUTELY AM. That is first and of infinite importance. Names are extremely significant in scripture. They are intended to reveal something about the person whose name it is. GOD IS HIS BEING. LORD IS HIS NAME.

(Exodus 15:11)

"Who is like you, O Lord, among the gods? Who is like you, majestic in holiness, awesome in glorious deeds, doing wonders?

(Psalms 66:5)

"Come and see what God has done: he is awesome in his deeds toward the children of man"

(Nehemiah 1:5)
"And I said, "O Lord God of heaven, the great and awesome God who keeps covenant and steadfast love with those who love him and keep his commandments."

Seeing that God wanted Moses to know who he was before he told him his name, gave God pleasure in revealing himself. From the marble halls of the palace in Egypt, dressed with the finest clothing of that day with custom made jewelry around his neck and on his wrists, eating the best foods available, being an educated orator... to someone who is **now** 80 years of age, stutters in his speech, living as a nomad, attending sheep and stepping in sheep dung. God gets his attention in the desert by having a bush on fire, yet not being consumed for the sole purpose of revealing his awesomeness. I cannot but think that if God wanted that for Moses, I believe that HE wants that for you as well. Maybe not to the extreme that it took for Moses, but I believe that God in his wisdom, allows certain situations that are tailor made just for you to get your attention. I believe that God desires to convey something between us and Him... His Awesomeness. How is this done?

On a normal Sunday morning, many wake up from their slumber from Saturday night, rising to another day with no expectations that God will meet them at the point of their need. Going through the routine of attending service for the sake of consciousness, they may feel good by knowing that they were there. Yet Sunday after Sunday, many gather just to leave out as they came in, untouched, unchanged, and uninspired. In fact, many believe God is boring. Yes, I know that attending some church services can be very lifeless and empty. I've talked to many people that will not have anything to do with a church service and, to some degree, I understand. But on the other hand, I must say in understanding that it causes me to realize that they have not had an encounter just yet with God regarding his awesomeness. Yes, church services can be boring and ritualistic, but when you have an encounter with God, in seeing who He is, your whole perspective changes. Seeing Him, changes you. In fact, according to the scriptures, whenever a person had an encounter with God, they were visibly shaken and changed.

When Moses saw God at the burning bush, he hid his face and trembled. When Isaiah saw the Lord high and lifted up, he cried, "Woe is me, I am undone; for my eyes have seen the King, the Lord of Host." When Jesus appeared to Saul on the road to Damascus, on the ground, he was in fear and trembling. When the Apostle John saw him on the island of Patmos, he fell as one dead. My point is, you cannot see him and not be affected. Your experience may not be as intense as these, but be assured, you will be profoundly affected. The scriptures are filled with those who saw him in different fashions and were forever changed. Is He not the same today? Your whole perspective will change and your whole way of life will never be the same. What is perspective? It is a mental view or outlook. It is a particular evaluation of something. When there is evaluation, you set the value of something or you determine the significance, worth, or quality of it. Since we are not talking about an inanimate object but talking about God, what is your outlook or view of Him?

What's your value of Him and how significant is He to you? I believe that the only way you can answer these questions is to have an encounter with Him. It takes just one glimpse of His glory, one touch of his power, just one experience of the embracing of his love, and you will be changed forever. I will never forget the day that I had my first encounter with Him. Over 40 years ago, though it seems like just yesterday, my life was forever changed. I was seventeen years of age, raised in a large family, attending church every Sunday as far as I could remember. At the age of 9, I remember that my father was the pastor of Second Baptist Church in Reno, Nevada, and my mother was the pianist. After a year in Reno, my father suddenly became ill and passed away. That left a gaping hole in my heart that no one could fill. My mother, having to raise five boys and three girls, decided to move us back to Sacramento, California. We reunited with the church in Sacramento and served there. Music was and still is a large part of our lives. My father was a singer as well as a pastor, and my mother was trained in the art of classical music and gospel. How we enjoyed her playing. In light of this, we were very involved in the music department of the church. One of my brothers directed and the other played, and we were all heavily occupied with music. However, as much as I enjoyed music, and enjoyed singing, I was so empty inside. Going to church every Sunday and participating in service left me totally unsatisfied. I was so unsatisfied that I began to get involved with marijuana and other drugs, to the point that I would bring them to church and get high. That's how boring and empty and unsatisfied I was. During service, I would slip out into the fellowship hall, take my drugs, and then go back into the choir stand and trip, if you know what I mean! I did this for about two years of my life, going through the routine of church, home, and school.

Week after week, month after month, until something wonderful happened to me – I had an encounter with Him. On a Thursday night, in the month of August 1971, on the corner of 35th and Broadway in Sacramento, California, in an old theater building, I met Him for the first time in a revival service that my next-door neighbor invited me to. I sang about him, read about him, talked about him, called myself serving him, but I came to find out that I was dead inside, no spiritual life at all. I was empty, disgusted, unsatisfied, lonely, and bored with life, having no purpose. I literally did not know what I was living for, until... I SAW HIM! I really saw him and met Him in a way that I will never forget. I did not see the heavens open up and see his throne. I saw no angels; I heard no audible voice from heaven. The earth did not shake, the thunder did not roll, and I jumped over no pews, but I SAW HIM, and my life was never the same. I encountered one of the greatest things I could ever know of Him...HIS LOVE, which he had for me. He knew me. He understood what I was going through and had gone through in my life. I did not have to tell him anything about me, He just knew. He looked beyond my faults and saw and met my need, and my need was Him. He was the one that filled the loneliness in my heart. He healed the wounds that life dealt to me. He filled that gaping hole in my heart that was left by the passing of my father, and He brought excitement into my life. He brought complete satisfaction, for he is the only one that can satisfy a soul. And most of all, he gave me purpose.

There I was on the altar, being saturated by his presence and engulfed in his love. He put his arms around me, and I just melted into his arms because I felt so safe and secure in him. I knew that everything was going to be alright because now I had Him, and He had me. I saw him. I saw and experienced his love. His love is beyond human words of expression. I cannot begin to express to you how wonderful his love is, but if I tried, I would say he is Awesome. My whole entire perspective in life changed in a moment after seeing him. At 17 years old, I had this first encounter with him, with many more that followed that took me from one level to the next in seeing who He is. Now I'm 68 and after 50 years of walking with Him, He is as fresh now as He was then. As the word says, "He is the same yesterday, today, and forever. He never changes. He just gets greater in experience as the years go by. Oh, how wonderful it was to encounter Him. I can truly say that He is awesome. There is one thing everyone has in common when they encounter Him, and that is you may not be able to remember the date or all the circumstances, but you will never forget the experience. He is extremely impressive, and I have an overwhelming feeling of reverence and admiration for Him, for He truly is Astonishing, Breathtaking, Magnificent, Wonderful, Majestic, and Amazing.

When you first have an encounter with Him, I have found that there are other ways to experience Him. When people have an encounter with Him, there is one thing they all have in common, a thankful heart filled with praise. I believe it is impossible to encounter him and not praise Him, for praise springs up from the depth of the soul in a very dramatic way. David said:

(Psalm 69:30)
"I will praise the name of God with a song; I will magnify him with thanksgiving".

There are many passages in scripture concerning praise. Praise is a wonderful thing to do. In fact, the Lord commands us to praise Him. Have you ever wondered why? Why are there so many commands to praise Him?

What benefit is there in praising Him? Many have asked the same questions. In fact, there was a man by the name of C.S. Lewis who knew about these commands, yet he stumbled over them. It was said, "That as he was beginning to believe in God, he faced a great stumbling block, which was the presence of demands scattered throughout the Psalms that he should praise God." He did not see the point in all this; besides, it seemed to picture God as craving "for our worship like a vain woman who wants compliments."

There are many people in the secular world who believe that God has an ego problem; that His commands in the Bible are there to, as we would say, "to stroke His ego." That is so far from the truth. Others believe that the only reason we were created was because God was lonely. Let it be known that God is not in need of our praise nor our worship. It adds nothing to who he already is. God was never in need of anything or anyone, and never will be. Yet, C.S. Lewis goes on to show why he was wrong:

"But the most obvious fact about praise—whether of God or anything—strangely escaped me. I thought of it in terms of compliment, approval, or the giving of honor. I had never noticed that all enjoyment spontaneously overflows into praise.... The world rings with praise— lovers praising their mistresses, readers their favorite poet, walkers praising the countryside, players praising their favorite game... I think we delight to praise what we enjoy because the praise not merely expresses but completes the enjoyment; it is its appointed consummation." Even Johnathan Edwards stated,

God glorifies Himself toward us in two ways:

1. By appearing to our understanding.

2. In communicating Himself to our hearts, and in our rejoicing and delighting in, and enjoying the manifestations which He makes of Himself.... God is glorified not only by His glory being seen, but by his glory being enjoyed.

I believe that is the key. We praise what we enjoy. God is pleased not only by our wonder of His awesomeness, but also by us enjoying His awesomeness. You see, praise is not for God, it is for us. Seeing who He is takes our focus off ourselves and our circumstances, and we begin to see how great He is. His awesomeness is for us because the more we see Him, the more we are changed. He is all we need for complete satisfaction. So having an encounter with God is the greatest thing anybody could ever experience, and when you do, your heart will explode with praise because He is so...AWE-SOME.

CHAPTER 2

Who are you that He would have you in mind?

(Psalms 8:3-4 ERV)

"I look at the heavens you made with your hands. I see the moon and the stars you created. And I wonder, "Why are people so important to you? Why do you even think about them? Why do you care so much about humans? Why do you even notice them?"

I remember it well, on a late summer night in my early teen years, laying on the warm concrete driveway of the home I grew up in, starring up at the midnight sky. My eyes were fixed on the many stars that shined from the black, backdrop of night. "How beautiful they are", I thought, "like diamonds reflecting their brilliance." There were so many that I could not count them all *(and I really tried counting the stars I was looking at).* Some stars were shining more brightly than others, yet all were wonderful, and it seemed that they were so close to each other. As I continued to gaze, I saw several shooting stars streak across the sky, leaving tails of light as they disappeared into the night sky. Still being engaged with it all, I became overwhelmed with the beauty of the night, and suddenly, at the same time, I began to feel very insignificant. Questions began to rise up from my very soul asking, "Why am I here? Why do I have this consciousness of being? Why do I have this conscience about myself? What am I here for and why was I born? I felt so small, so tiny in comparison to what I was observing. It was the strangest feeling I ever had, but in a very powerful way, it got my attention. It caused me to really think about my existence.

Reading what David wrote in Psalms 8:3-4, I understood what he felt. I will never forget in the month of August 1981, shortly after I was married, I had to go back on the road headed toward Arizona to the White Mountain Apache Reservation for some revival meetings. It was exciting going back to Arizona because the people loved us, and we loved them. We had so many great times there and many lives were changed, from the young to adults. Those were very precious times that I will never forget, for they impacted my life in a very powerful way. We stayed in cabins back in the wooded area without phones or cell phones *(I do wonder how we made it in those days without cell phones)*. What a beautiful place high up in the mountains, peaceful and quiet, a place so quiet that you could hear the swishing sound of a crow's wings when it flew. There were times that we would open the window of the cabin to feed the animals popcorn. It was amazing to me because when we started to throw out the popcorn, there were only a few birds that would fly around and pick them up, but as we continued, it seemed like the whole forest of animals started coming toward the cabin. Squirrels would literally come up to the window and get the popcorn from my hand (*I felt like Adam*). It was so peaceful that I would take daily walks and enjoy the presence of God. There is nothing like spending time in the mountains with God and enjoying His presence. However, at night it was so dark that without the shining of the moon, I could not see my hand in front of my face. That was not the best feeling out there in the woods, if you know what I mean! I did not know what animals were staring at me in the dark or if I was being stalked. Why was I out there? Since we did not have phones in the cabins, we had to walk approximately a quarter of a mile to the front office where they had phone booths. It was the only place I could call my wife, whom I missed very much. As I started toward the front office, I could not proceed until my eyes adjusted to the darkness so I could see the shape of the road. Walking very slowly and nervously, I reached my destination and had a great time talking to my wife yet understanding that being there in the light of the office area and in the phone booth, my eyes had to re-adjust to the darkness all over again. So, there I was, heading back down this very dark path (*the things you do for love!*) But as I headed back, something wonderful happened to me. In the middle of going back, the thought came to my mind very strongly, "Look up," and when I did, it seemed like my breath was almost taken away. The stars! Oh, the stars! I was overwhelmed by the beauty of the night sky. I had never in my entire life seen so many stars. It wasn't like the experience of laying on the driveway where I grew up. In the city, you lose the wonderful sight of many stars because of the city lights but going out of the city to the country or up in the mountains, you will see stars like you have never seen. The Milky Way was absolutely gorgeous, and again I had the overwhelming feeling of my existence, but this time with much more clarity. I understood why I was here. I believe David was saying, *"When I consider or look on the heavens you have made the moon and stars, Who am "I"* ***that you would even think about me?*** *Who am I that you would even visit me?*

In the morning when I wake up, before I roll out of bed, before reading my emails or reading the latest headline news, I will begin my day by reading my devotions. Devotion is simply an act of prayer or private worship. It's a strong dedication to someone or something to which one is bound by. Being dedicated to private devotions first thing in the morning has its reward. Pastor John Piper, who I respect and admire very greatly, has devotional subject matters every day of the year on an app called "Solid Joys." His writings are, if I could explain it in these words, "simple, yet with great depth." As it was one morning, he was expounding on a passage that I referred to in Chapter One.

(Psalms 69:30)

"I will praise the name of God with a song; I will __magnify__ him with thanksgiving."

Pastor John Piper wrote,

"There are two kinds of magnifying: microscope magnifying and telescope magnifying. The one makes a small thing look bigger than it is. The other makes a big thing look as big as it really is. When David says, "I will magnify God with thanksgiving," he does not mean, "I will make a small God look bigger than he is." He means, "I will make a big God begin to look as big as he really is." We are not called to be microscopes. We are called to be telescopes...but you cannot magnify what you haven't seen."

God in who he is, is no small matter. Having an encounter with Him is like seeing him through telescope eyes. Allow me at this time to be a telescope in light of the title of this chapter. Have YOU ever considered the heavens, the works of His hands, the moon, and the stars? It is the most amazing thing to consider. It blows you away, as we would say. Consider these few facts:

1. Astronomers speculate that the universe is approximately 20 billion light years across. One light year is 186,000 miles per second. Meaning, it would take, if they are correct, 20 billion years to

cross the universe at the speed of 186,000 miles per second.

2. Our sun is one of at least 100 billion stars just in the Milky Way. Scientists calculate that there are at least 100 billion galaxies in the observable universe, each one brimming with stars. There are more stars than grains of sand on all of Earth's beaches combined *(just think, He knows them all by name)*.

3. Galaxies are huge collections of stars. They usually contain several million to over a trillion stars and can range in size from a few thousand to several hundred thousand light-years across. There are hundreds of billions of galaxies in the universe. Galaxies come in many different sizes, shapes, and brightness's.

4. The Milky Way is a huge city of stars, so big that even at the speed of light (186,000 miles per second), it would take 100,000 years to travel across it.

5. If the sun were as tall as a typical front door, Earth would be the size of a nickel.

6. Some stars are 600,000 times as bright as our sun.

7. All of the stars comprising the Milky Way galaxy revolve around the center of the galaxy once every 200 million years or so.

8. The stars that we see in the night sky, many of which are galaxies, that seem so close to each other, are actually millions of light years away from each other.

In light of these amazing facts and there are numerous more, it is no wonder why a scholar by the name of George Rawlinson once noted that,

"The thought that God who made the heavens should have such regard for humanity "is well-nigh overwhelming. He goes on to say that rather than suggesting that man is but an insignificant speck in the Universe, the passage in (Genesis 1:26) reveals that the Lord has bestowed a signal honor upon him who is in his very image."

Who are you that He would have you in mind? You are someone very special in His eyes and you are eternally loved. In light of what George Rawlinson said, I would like to change what he said in my own words:

"The thought that the God who made the heavens and the stars thereof would consider YOU is overwhelming."

It's overwhelming when you see God's perspective concerning you. As God told Jeremiah, he says the same to you.

(Jeremiah 1:5 MSG)
"Before I shaped you in the womb, I knew all about you. Before you saw the light of day, I had holy plans for you..."

David wrote in:

(Psalms 139:1-6; 13-18)

"LORD, you have examined me and you know me. You know everything I do; from far away you understand all my thoughts. You see me, whether I am working or resting; you know all my actions. Even before I speak, you already know what I will say. You are all round me on every side; you protect me with your power. Your knowledge of me is too deep; it is beyond my understanding."

"You created every part of me; you put me together in my mother's womb. I praise you because you are to be feared; all you do is strange and wonderful. I know it with all my heart. When my bones were being formed, carefully put together in my mother's womb, when I was growing there in secret, you knew that I was there — you saw me before I was born. The days allotted to me had all been recorded in your book, before any of them ever began. O God, how difficult I find your thoughts; how many of them there are! If I counted them, they would be more than the grains of sand..."

When you stop and meditate on this passage, you have to realize that you are not a mistake. You are not an accident. While you were in your mother's womb, God was knitting you together according to the DNA He ascribed to you: your color, your height, your temperament, your passions, your gifting, and so much more. He also appointed the means by which you would get here. We are able to make many choices in life, but there is one choice that we have no say so over and that is who our parents would be. You did not come from your parents; you came through your parents. You came from God. He had you in mind from eternity and sent you into this world through the canal of your mother's womb. I do realize that some of our arrivals were not the most pleasant. Some of us had very bad, hurtful, abusive experiences. Sometimes, we just cannot make heads or tails of why we had to come into this world having those experiences. I do not believe that it was God's will for anyone of us to have gone through what we experienced because His Word speaks of how we are to treat one another, how parents' ought to love and treat their children. But I also understand that God is sovereign, and nothing happens without his knowledge of it. As Paul said in:

(Romans 11:33-36)

"God's riches, wisdom, and knowledge are so deep that it is impossible to explain his decisions or to understand his ways. "Who knows how the Lord thinks? Who can become his adviser?" Who gave the Lord something which the Lord must pay back? Everything is from him and by him and for him. Glory belongs to him forever! Amen!"

Why did he permit these things? Why did he allow many of us to suffer at the hands of people? We do not **fully** understand or comprehend it, but as Joseph told his brothers, "You meant it for evil, but God meant it for good." Even Jesus stated in:

(Luke 12:7)
"But even the very hairs of your head are all numbered."

He did not say your hairs were counted but numbered. There is a difference. Counted means, "to determine the number of." But numbered means, "The action of creating or assigning for identification." The average human head has about 100,000 hair follicles. Each follicle can grow about 20 individual hairs in a person's lifetime. Average hair loss is around 100 strands a day. Yet, each strand of hair on your head is numbered for identification. Each one that falls to the ground when you comb your hair or comes out in your brush is numbered. God is aware that hair strand number 2,562, hair strand number 6,872, and 10,986 have fallen. Maybe you are one of those who have no hair at all. Know this, that He was aware of the last strand that fell from your head. In order to keep account of that which has identification, you have to be close to it or very accountable of it. That's how close God is to you. He's so close that he is aware of each strand that falls. Talk about micro-management! When you consider God's macro-management of the universe, the stars, and the ever-growing expansion of galaxies, it is so overwhelming to think He has you in mind, micro-managing your everyday life, which is of extreme importance to Him because He sees you in your future and you look better in your future than you look right now.

Who are you that He would have you in mind? His thoughts concerning you are as innumerable as the grains of sand. You can't count the thoughts **God** has about you, but you can know that what he is thinking is always to do you good!

CHAPTER 3

God's Intent for your life

"For I know the thoughts that I think toward you, says the LORD, thoughts of peace and not of evil, to give you a future and a hope."
(Jeremiah 29:11 NKJV)

"When things don't go as you would like them to go in your life, it doesn't mean that God has stopped doing you good. It means He is shifting things around to do you more good."

Looking into the background of this passage in Jeremiah 29:11, the Jewish nation was in Babylon for seventy years, being held captive for forsaking the law of their God. They were warned time after time that they would be removed from the land if they continued in their idolatry. They were told by the prophets that God would give them victory concerning the armies that surrounded them, and they should not be afraid. But God sent a different message through the Prophet Jeremiah, and the people refused to adhere to the warning, and for this reason they suffered greatly. Israel had a history of faithfulness and unfaithfulness, yet God was always faithful and never wavered in fulfilling the promises He spoke concerning them. He did exactly what He said He would do after 70 years of captivity.

God raised up King Cyrus for the sole purpose of benefiting His people. Being God's people, I'm sure they could not see through all the pain and suffering they were encountering, but God is faithful. *"Faithful is He that promised" (Hebrews 10:23).*

While in captivity in Babylon, God was shifting things around to do them better. Yes, He was always at work, even when they did not see it or believe it. For they said, *"How can we sing the Lord's song in a strange land, so they hung their harps on the willow tree"* (Psalms 137:1-4).

They did not realize that God's intent for them was "good." He was in the process of shifting things around for the purpose of achieving what He desired to do for them, bringing them into a better place and position which He could bless them much more. Why? Because God had a plan and despite their rebellion, they were His people, and He loved them. There is something about the love of God that is so amazing that the Greeks had to come up with a word to describe it, "AGAPE". Its meaning is used to describe the love that is of and from God, whose very nature is love. *"God is love" (1 John 4:8).* Everything God does flows from His love. God loves because that is His nature and the expression of His being. He loves the unlovable and the unlovely. Not because they deserve to be loved or because of any excellence they possess, but because it is His nature to love. You see, God was always thinking about them, and His intention or purpose was to do them good. But God's purpose for them had to include "process." They could not have God's purpose without God's process. They go together. What good is process without there being a purpose? Process prepares you for purpose. There cannot be any fulfillment of purpose without process, for the process gets you ready for purpose. Process is the series of events leading up to an end result; a series of actions that produce something... PURPOSE! If there is no purpose, there will be no process.

"Therefore, we do not lose heart. Even though our outward man is perishing, (PROCESS) Yet the inward man is being renewed day by day. (PURPOSE) For our light affliction, which is but for a moment, (PROCESS) is working for us a far more exceeding and eternal weight of glory, (PURPOSE) While we do not look at the things which are seen, (PROCESS) but at the things which are not seen. (PURPOSE) For the things which are seen are temporary, (PROCESS) but the things which are not seen are eternal." (PURPOSE)
II Corinthians 4:16-18 NKJV

"The Spirit Himself bears witness with our spirit that we are children of God, and if children, then heirs—heirs of God and joint heirs with Christ, (PURPOSE) if indeed we suffer with Him, (PROCESS) that we may also be glorified together. (PURPOSE) For I consider that the sufferings of this present time.(PROCESS) are not

worthy to be compared with the glory which shall be revealed in us." (PURPOSE)
Romans 8:16-18 NKJV

Your process is not your purpose!

When we consider the people used by God throughout the Bible, it may appear that they are somewhat like Super Men or Super Women. It also may appear that the events that happen to these biblical characters occur in a speedy manner, however it would benefit us to look at their lives through the eyes of a 24-hour window or time frame. We must not look at the events concerning their lives with a *"Micro-Wave Mentality"*. We have to understand that they were regular human beings as we are today. They saw the same sun rise and set, they saw the same moon with the same cycles, and the constellations of the stars that we see today. They have been there for thousands of years, and the process that God sent His people through took time. Minute by minute, hour by hour, month by month, and year by year. In this day and time, we are in a hurry for everything. We want things *"Right Now!"* I believe that technology has spoiled us, and we expect God to adapt to the times of *"Right Now."* But God will not adapt to our impatience. He will not adapt to our micro-wave mentality. He will not adapt to our "name it and claim it" and "get it tomorrow" precepts. He will not adapt to, as we quote so many times, "God hastens to perform his word," declaration. He will not adapt to our, "speak it into the atmosphere," and quickly you will have it. No, we have to wait on God, and adapt to the realization that His time is not our time, and He moves as He pleases in His time. I know that there are times we say God is waiting on us, and that is true in certain circumstances, but even though we get in place, we still have to wait.

So, it was with Abraham. God spoke to him to leave his country and He would lead him to a land and make his name great. His descendants would be as the stars in heaven and as the sand of the seashore, yet he had no offspring at the age of 75, for Sarah was barren. The process began and lasted for 25 years before fulfillment. Abraham waited patiently. Then he received the promise, being 100 years old.

So, it was with David. Anointed to be king as an adolescent by Samuel, yet the fulfillment of his reign did not begin until the age of 30. The process took approximately 15 years or so.

So, it was with Moses. Commissioned to go to Egypt to lead them out. The process took 80 years of his life.

So, it was with Joseph. God gave him two dreams at the age of 17 concerning the purpose God had for Him. The process took 13 years before he began to rule.

The only difference between their day and ours is that we have technology and they did not. Nevertheless, we are human, with human weaknesses and sin, not X-Men, or The Avengers, or The Black

Panther, or The Gifted, or the Fantastic Four, and last but not least, Captain America! There are many, many more that God left on record for us to study and observe. While they were in process, they could not fully see that God's purpose was being worked out in their lives, for I believe that they too wondered how long, because God did not speak every day to them. Sometimes God's voice was heard a few years in between while in the process. Reading about their lives, we see that there were many times when things were not so good. As Jacob once cried out, *"All these things are against me."* But we also see how God, at the end of the day, worked out all things for their good according to His purpose. *"Since God is for us, who can successfully be against us?"* (Romans 8:31 AMP). God will not turn away from doing us good. It was God's way for them, and it is God's way today.

So, can we personally apply to our lives what God said to Israel in Jeremiah 29:11? Absolutely! Though this is a different time, God is still God and His principles never change. What is "principle?" It is a fundamental truth that serves as the foundation for a system of behavior. God is Holy, Just, and Wise in all of His ways. He uses the best means to bring about the best results. Those of you who are walking through tough times in your lives, please know this: *"God's been thinking about you and His intent is ALWAYS to do you GOOD!* Always? Yes, always. God has always thought about you in a very loving way.

How many times have you heard someone say, "Isn't this a coincidence? I was just thinking about you, and you called." This happens many times in our lives. People that come across our minds while we are busy during the day, that we have not seen or talked to in a while, and wonder where they are or what they're doing, end up showing up or getting in contact with us. That is a very delightful experience, and we are amazed when this happens. When we think about it, the odds of that happening on its own are baffling because of the details that go along with it. We use the word coincidence when we can't explain how or the timing of something happening like this unexpectedly.

God's thoughts about you and what you are walking through are not a coincidence. I believe this is one of the most difficult things for us to accept and comprehend. Many of us are walking through some very tough times in our lives, things that make no sense when we look at life from our own perspective. Contrary to what some believe, Christians are not exempt from suffering. As much as we do not enjoy suffering, we will never get away from it in this life. *"Many are the afflictions of the righteous, but the Lord shall deliver them out of them all (Psalms 34:19).*

The word "affliction" is defined as, *"Anything that causes pain, distress, grief, misfortune, sickness, loss, calamity, mental or bodily pain."* As a believer in this world, there is no escape from the suffering of process.

There is always suffering in process. David said, "My times are in your hand." The hand of God exemplifies His power. It doesn't matter how much suffering you are walking through; no suffering is greater than His hand. He is able to do a "suddenly" in your life at any moment. He is in complete control of your situations. There are believers in this world that are going through pain, sorrow, misfortune, emotional distress, abuse, lack, poverty, incurable diseases, sickness, the death of loved ones, persecutions, imprisonment, being accused of crimes they did not commit, abandonment, etc. But these sufferings do not make them unbelievers. It doesn't mean they have a lack of faith or their faith is not strong enough or they have weak faith. No! On the contrary, it means just the opposite. Many of us overlook what is written in the book of Hebrews in Chapter 11, better known as "The Hall of Faith." As you begin to read this chapter, you get victory after victory of those who God used, especially when you get to verse 32-35. But verses 36-40 brings another side of the coin.

"AND OTHERS" experienced the trial of mocking and scourging [amid torture], and even chains and imprisonment.

They were stoned [to death], they were sawn in two, they were lured with tempting offers [to renounce their faith], they were put to death by the sword; they went about wrapped in the skins of sheep and goats, utterly destitute, oppressed, cruelly treated (People of whom the world was not worthy), wandering in deserts and mountains and [living in] caves and holes in the ground.

And all of these, though they gained [divine] approval through their faith, did not receive [the fulfillment of] what was promised,

Because God had us in mind and had something better for us, so that they [these men and women of authentic faith] would not be made perfect [that is, completed in Him] apart from us."

We tend to forget about those two words, "and others." One thing I came to realize is that you cannot "*Americanize the Gospel.*" *It is not an American book written after or according to American customs.* As the character Forest Gump would say, "*That's all I have to say about that.*"

As long as believers are in this world, there will be times or seasons of suffering. Jesus told us that in this world we shall have tribulation, but be of good courage, I have overcome the world" (John 16:33). In this world, you are a believer by the grace of God. He chose you before the foundation of the world. He did not choose you to lose you in the midst of your suffering. Jesus himself said,

"All whom My Father gives (entrusts) to Me will come to Me; and the one who comes to Me I will most certainly not cast out [I will never, no never, reject one of them who comes to Me]. For I have come down from heaven not to do My own will and purpose but to do the will and purpose of Him Who sent Me. And this is the will of Him

Who sent Me, that I should not lose any of all that He has given Me" (John 6:37-39 AMPC).

Note: I encourage you to read and re-read these verses with a prayerful and meditative heart, it will change your life.

Remember, you are walking through this; you are not parked. This is not your permanent status; this is only temporary. He is taking you somewhere, and that somewhere is His purpose for your life. There is movement even though it seems like you are at a standstill. You must trust Him when you can't trace Him. As I stated earlier, "When things don't go as you would like them to, it doesn't mean that God has stopped doing you good; it only means He is shifting things around to do you more good." What do I mean by shifting things around? He is changing and moving things around not only in your situations or circumstances but within you as well, in order to achieve a desired result. This is exactly what God is doing pertaining to Romans 8:28, and it states,

"For we know that God causes all things to work together for the good to them who love God and are the called according to His Purpose."

We hear and quote this verse so many times that I believe that we have missed its weightiness. It is a very weighty verse, much weightier than we realize. Since God's intention is to do us good, I believe that this verse speaks to us in a way far deeper than we can imagine. I realize there are other verses that relate to this verse, but since we are dealing with the title of this book, *God's Been Thinking About You*, I believe this verse is the heartstring of this book, so I would like to investigate this a little more than usual. I believe that the first three words of this verse is essential for us to see and understand the remainder of it, "For We Know."

Paul is making a declaration that we KNOW this. It is as though he is saying we already know this within our hearts without fully understanding it. This is common knowledge that's been placed in us. Although we know the following truth *intuitively*, we may not always fully understand and sense it *experientially*. Dr. Torrey once said that this verse is a "soft pillow for a tired heart." And as someone else said, "God's promises put a rainbow of hope in every cloud and a "pillow of grace" in every bed of affliction!" God promised us that no matter what the process brings, whether good or bad, sweet or bitter, sunshine or rain, light or darkness, victory or defeat, He's going to cause it to work toward or to produce good from it. We are to KNOW THIS!

Let's go further. We're here so that the purpose of God might be worked out in our lives. He is the *"Purpose Giver"* and the *"Purpose Worker."* When you look at this verse closer, the words "Sovereignty" and "Providence" are wonderfully seen. Sovereignty is defined as *"having total control of all things past, present, and future."* Nothing happens that is out of His knowledge and control. All things are either caused by Him or allowed by Him for His own purposes and through His perfect will and timing (Romans 11:36). He is the only absolute and omnipotent ruler of the universe and is unrestricted in His supremacy. He is sovereign in creation, providence, and redemption.

Providence is defined as:

"Supplying what is needed. It is to see on behalf of. "See to" means "take care of, provide for." **In other words, it is seeing something with purpose and making provision for what is seen.** *It is "providing." It is the act of God sustaining and governing the universe."*

God causes all things according to His purpose. Realizing this will cause us to see that He gives purpose "sovereignly." Because ultimately, all things are for His purpose, which works good in our lives. He is Sovereign over all things and at all times. His Providence is working powerfully even when our world seems to be falling apart! The comforting truth of Romans 8:28 is based especially on God's sovereignty. If all things work together for good (all events, all circumstances, all trials, etc.), then it follows that God must be over all things and must control all things. This is not fatalism. This is the wonderful fact that God, in all His wisdom and love, is in complete control of it all! *Sovereignly*, it is God that causes all things... according to His purpose, which *Providentially* works things for good, for our benefit, profit, and advantage. David says in:

(Psalms 23:6)
"Surely goodness and mercy shall follow me all the days of my life."

The verse should read, *"Surely Goodness and Mercy shall "Pursue" me all the days of my life..."* Pursue means to, "Run after, to carry on or continue a course of action." Is it any wonder that Paul would write?

(Ephesians 2:10)
"For we are God's masterpiece. He has created us anew in Christ Jesus, so we can do the good things he planned for us long ago." **NLT**

"For we are His workmanship [His own master work, a work of art], created in Christ Jesus [reborn from above--spiritually transformed, renewed, ready to be used] for good works, which God prepared [for us] beforehand [taking paths which He set], so that we would walk in them [living the good life which He prearranged and made ready for us]." **AMP**

We all are unique in our own special way because God has made us uniquely different giving each of us His own purpose which He works out in us.

(Philippians 2:13) NLT
"For God is working in you, giving you the desire and the power to do what pleases him."

At the beginning of the year, sometimes going old school, I went to the store to buy a calendar for making plans and for keeping up with things that were to come. As I unwrapped the cellophane to look at my calendar, I noticed that there was a thin piece of cardboard in the back of the calendar made by Day Spring. To my surprise, there was a message written on the cardboard by co-founder, Roy Lessin, that I would like to end this chapter with.

JUST THINK,
You're here not by chance,
But by God's choosing.
His hand formed you
And made you
The person you are.
He compares you to no one else-
You are one of a kind.
You lack nothing
That His grace can't give you.
He has allowed you to be here
At this time in history
To fulfill His special purpose
For this generation.

"To everything there is a season, and a time to every purpose under the heaven:"
Ecclesiastes 3:1 KJV

CHAPTER 4

Your response to God's intention for your life

There he was in agony of heart and mind, wondering why he had to bear this pain, this affliction, this suffering. He could not understand having asked the Lord to take it from him that it had not departed. Did not Jesus say if you ask it will be given, seek and you will find, knock and it will be opened unto you? For he who asks, receives. He who seeks, finds, and he that knocks the door will be opened? Then WHY hadn't the Lord answered? What's taking Him so long to respond? Looking over his life he began to think about what he had gone through:

"*Imprisonments, beaten times without number, and often in danger of death. Five times he received from the Jews thirty-nine lashes. Three times he was beaten with rods once he was stoned. Three times he was shipwrecked, a night and a day he spent adrift on the sea; many times on journeys, [exposed to] danger from rivers, danger from bandits, danger from his own countrymen, danger from the Gentiles, danger in the city, danger in the wilderness, danger on the sea, danger among those posing as believers; in labor and hardship, often unable to sleep, in hunger and thirst, often [driven to] fasting [for lack of food], in cold and exposure [without adequate clothing]. Besides those external things, there is the daily [inescapable] pressure of his concern for all the churches...*" and yet having to bear *this added affliction that was given to him which strikes him from without, this thorn in the flesh, this messenger of Satan.*

He sought the Lord three times for Him to take this away from him. We don't know exactly what it was, but we know that God had a purpose for it, and what was the purpose? Lest he became too exalted in his own mind because of the abundance of the revelations that was given to him. But the day came that the Lord finally answered him. He said, "My grace is sufficient for you: for my strength is made perfect in weakness." In other words:

"My grace is sufficient for you [My lovingkindness and My mercy are more than enough--always available--regardless of the situation]; for [My] power is being perfected [and is completed and shows itself most effectively] in [your] weakness."

Then He said something very interesting:

Therefore, I will all the more gladly boast in my weaknesses, so that the power of Christ [may completely enfold me and] may dwell in me." "So, I am well pleased with weaknesses, with insults, with distresses, with persecutions, and with difficulties, for the sake of Christ; for when I am weak [in human strength], then I am strong [truly able, truly powerful, truly drawing from God's strength]."

What happened to Him to make him say, "Therefore most gladly I will rather boast in my infirmities, that the power of Christ may rest upon me?"

I'll tell you what happened: "HE HAD AN ATTITUDE ADJUSTMENT," a powerful, life-changing shift in his mindset. Paul changed his entire outlook. The new attitude gave him a change of heart and mind, resulting in a new attitude. *Attitude* is a state of mind in regards to something or someone. *Attitude* is the way you think and feel about it, especially when this shows in the way you behave.

It had much to do with his attitude. The attitude we take to the thing that troubles us. We might like it to depart, but God may elect that it should stay. You see, your attitude makes the difference. God is very concerned about how we think. Many people say, "I want to change." They express their desire for things to be different, thinking that suddenly just by their request things will change. You know as well as I do that it is not that easy. There is something we have to do and it starts with our attitude. If you don't have a changed mind, you will not change nor your situation because the changing of the situation starts with the changing of your attitude. The change must start with you inwardly.

Romans 12:2

"...Be transformed/changed by the renewing of your mind..."

Winston Churchill

"Attitude is a little thing that makes a big difference."

Zig Ziglar

"Your attitude, not your aptitude, will determine your altitude."

John Maxwell

"Positive thinking will not always change your circumstances, but it will always change you. Life is 10% of what happens to you and 90% of how you react to it."

Someone said, "If you don't like something, change it. If you can't change it, change your attitude."

Your response to God's purpose for your life is very important to the heart of God. When you respond to something or someone, you reply or react. How have you responded concerning God's purpose for your life, especially being in the process stage? What type of attitude have you responded with in your attitude about God's sovereign decision concerning yourself? In his book, *Stepping Into Greatness*, Dr. Mark Chironna made a statement and I quote,

"In the pursuit of our life's purpose, there will strategically occur a defining moment in the form of a refining crisis. In this refining crisis, God sets us free from

our confining limitations and empowers us to step into greatness."

I would like to say this in another way, yet not changing it's meaning.

In the pursuit of God's purpose for our lives, there will occur a defining or deciding moment...which will be strategic on God's part...and if we make the right decisions...God will set us free from limitations...and empower us to step into his purpose.

When I think about this statement, my mind immediately **goes** to the children of Israel on their way to the promised land. God's purpose for them was to possess the land that He had given them, but they had not arrived yet. God could have taken them a shorter route, but He took them another way. Approximately an 11-day trip turned into a 40-year journey. He took them that way to test them to see what was in their hearts. We know God knows all things and nothing takes him by surprise. He knows our thoughts afar off. He is acquainted with all of our ways and knows our uprising and down-sitting (Psalms 139:1-4). It wasn't so much as God finding out what was in their hearts; He wanted them to see what was in their hearts. All that He did for them by displaying his great power and judgement on the gods of Egypt, yet during the process in the wilderness, they murmured and complained about their condition. God strategically took them through the wilderness. During the wilderness experience, they did not fully understand that God was preparing them for the fulfillment of His promise. It was a process, but they got struck in the process by their complaints and dissatisfaction with God and did not make it into the promise land. Their attitudes kept them out of the land, and they lived to regret it. They did not make the right decision concerning their attitudes toward God. The wilderness was a temporary limitation that they never got free from because of the way they thought. Had they made the right decision, God would have set them free from the crisis of the wilderness, into empowering them to enter into HIS purpose for their lives.

We can look at that generation of Israelites and say to ourselves, "We would have never done what they did after seeing all that God did for them to prove his faithfulness." Really? Human nature does not change. That which is born of the flesh is flesh. If you take the time and think about yourself, you will come to find out that you would have done the same thing many times over with your attitude. Our attitude toward God when we are in our processes, if we are not careful, will result in a negative attitude.

If we are not careful, we will begin to have the wrong attitude toward the way God **has** taken us and the way He **is** taking us. What do I mean by the way He has taken us? When you look back over your life, sometimes you just cannot fathom why God would allow you to have gone through what you had to endure. The hurt, pain, wounds, rejection, molestation, abusive relationships, addictions, adoption, imprisonments, being born into a family that wasn't really a family shaped you into making decisions that were not healthy for you and affected your whole life. We, at times, feel like we did not deserve that path. But who are we to complain to Him what should or should not have been? His wisdom is so in-depth that we will never be able to completely understand his decisions (Romans 11:33-36). But when you stop and think about it, you would never have been the person you are had you not gone through what you went through because it was not all about you but about someone else. What is your response concerning who you are, your temperament and God's sovereign decision about your life? John Maxwell stated:

"Until you make peace with who you are, you'll never be content with where you are."

If I may so boldly add:

*"Until you make peace with who you are, you'll never be content with where you are..."***and where you're headed."**

Which brings me to the expression, the way He is taking us. His ways are not our ways. The definition that I love about the wisdom of God is, "God uses the best means to bring about the best results." He knows what He's doing. He knows the best method to bring us to the end result. Your process was tailored made just for you. No one else will be able to fit the "size" of your process. From generation to generation, the Father works the same way. First, giving us His purpose and then sending us through the process that leads us to the manifestation of His purpose. He is the one who is taking us to the mountaintops and then through the valleys.

There is a word called "serendipity," which is defined as "finding pleasant things not looked for; finding valuable things unexpectedly and not sought for." In this word serendipity, there is found the word, "dip." This word is an interesting word that means, "to plunge momentarily." When God sends us through our process, there is something that keeps us motivated. Out of all that the process brings our way, why is it that we keep going and persevering in spite of? It is because God, unexpectedly to us at the time, dips us into His purpose for our lives, meaning He gives us a taste of our destiny, which is His purpose. He allows us to taste the sweetness of it at a time we least expect and allows us to swim in it and bathe in its glory. It is called a dream or vision. Then suddenly, he removes us out of it so that our palates would have had a full taste. We remember the experience as though tasting some delicate food for the first time, never to forget. This is what keeps us going forward despite the challenges of the process. What is your response after tasting your destiny and then being pulled out of it, only to realize that you have not yet reached God's purpose for your life? In reality, you are in the middle of God's means or methods which are not pleasant. What is your response when, in the middle of the process, you are being defeated or overwhelmed, or crushed by the weight of it all?

By nature, our reaction is one of fear, doubt, disbelief, discouragement, being dismayed, etc. But if we begin to see ourselves in God's perspective, through His word, there will be a response of not a bad attitude, but an attitude of praise and thanksgiving. Yes, I believe they are the key. Praise and thanksgiving send a message to God in a way nothing else does. It sends a message of faith to God in saying, "I will trust you in spite of what I see and feel. I will trust you in spite of what I do and do not understand." We praise Him for who He is, and we thank Him for what He has done and is going to do. In **1 Thessalonians 5:18 it reads:**

"In every situation [no matter what the circumstances] be thankful and continually give thanks to God; for this is the will of God for you in Christ Jesus." **AMP**

I will never forget one day as I was meditating over this verse, I asked myself what is the meaning behind the word 'thanks'? I came to find out that giving thanks indicates the obligation to someone for a favor done. Then I thought, God wants me to be thankful in everything, no exceptions. Thankful in every situation at all times and in every circumstance because He is doing me a favor by taking me through this process that he has ordered. When you are IN something, you are surrounded or enclosed by something. Life's circumstances enclose us, and these circumstances or situations many times are very uncomfortable for us as they press in on us, yet He says for us to have the attitude of thanksgiving in the midst of them. But we must always remember that we are not only surrounded by circumstances, but we are also surrounded by the God of circumstances. What do I mean? In 1 Peter 2:9, Peter states that we are a "peculiar" people, which means a "purchased" people. The word peculiar carries the idea of making a ring around something to mark it as one's own. Let me demonstrate. It is as if you have a sheet of paper and you draw a dot in the middle of the paper and then draw a circle around the dot. Outside of the circle are the situations of life with the purpose of getting to the dot within. This indicates that nothing can get to the dot without first crossing the line of the circle. Even so it is with our lives. We are surrounded not only by situations but also surrounded by the presence of God, meaning nothing can get to us without first passing through the will of God. The man Job, out of all that he went through, his pain, suffering and loss, said, "The Lord gives, and the Lord takes away. Blessed be the name of the Lord." I know that there is controversy over who did this to Job, but at the end of the day, God gave Satan permission to do what he did, yet God received the glory and restored back to Job double what he had before. God was doing Job a favor when he could not see or understand it. God was doing Joseph a favor when he allowed him to go through 13 years of suffering before his exaltation. This is why our attitude must be right. You cannot give thanks and complain at the same time; one will cancel out the other. Giving thanks is in the present, which calls for this to be our habitual attitude. Lack of thankfulness comes from pride, from the conviction that we deserve something better than we have, even though He is doing us a favor by allowing these things to come through His will.

Have you not asked yourself at one time or another, "Am I going to make it? I can't take no more of this. I can't take another step. I'm all prayed and fasted out. I'm having an Elijah and Jonah moment. What am I going to do? This is just too much for my life at this time. God, are you really with me? How long, oh Lord? My soul is cast down. My enemies have surrounded me in order to eat up my flesh. I can't take another step forward. I am tired and weary. God, do you hear my heart's cry?"

There have been times in our lives that we all have experienced these moments. These moments are not pleasant moments at all. There are times you want to go to sleep and not wake up. If you have not had these types of experiences or emotions, as my mother would say to me years ago as I was growing up, "keep living." Nevertheless, when these times come, He is always there. One of my favorite passages of scripture is **Isaiah 41:10, Amplified version,**

"Do not fear [anything], for I am with you; Do not be afraid, for I am your God. I will strengthen you, be assured I will help you; I will certainly take hold of you with My righteous right hand [a hand of justice, of power, of victory, of salvation].'"

Out of the midst of the processes of life, God does not want us to fear or get dismayed, which is defined as the emotion felt when one's expectations are not met, the cause of losing courage, or to break down the courage because of trouble. He does not want us to be fretful. He wants us to see Him for who He is. He desires for us to look not only at the present but in the past, eternity past. What do I mean? When Timothy was going through some church issues, Paul had to encourage him by reminding him of his calling and for him to stir up the gift of God which was in him by the laying on of his hands. For God did not give him the spirit of fear but of power, love, and a sound mind. Which brings me to **2 Timothy 1:9:**

*"Therefore do not be ashamed of the testimony about our Lord, nor of me his prisoner, but share in suffering for the gospel by the power of God, who saved us and called us to a holy calling, **not because of our works but because of his own purpose and grace, which he gave us in Christ Jesus before the ages began."***

Notice that "purpose" and "grace" were given to us before time began. I see this as though purpose and grace have been waiting on us to discover them before time began. If I may boldly say, *"Purpose is what is written in the books of heaven about you, and God has given Grace to be the empowerment to bring the purpose of God to pass."* God will not let the manifestation of purpose be without process and grace, for it takes the grace of God to be with you while being in the process. Grace will see you through. His grace is sufficient. Grace has been given to us to endure the process of the fulfillment of the purpose of God. So therefore, while you are in the midst of your process, headed toward your purpose, be thankful unto Him for having this assurance that He's been thinking about you, and His intent is to always do you good.

Faithful is He that will do it!

God's Thought

There are times in life that you may go through trials. You may often feel down and defeated, with thoughts that everyone, including God, has forgotten about you. During these times, it is important to believe and remember that God is in control, and He knows exactly what He is doing.

Jeremiah 29-11 says, *"For I know the plans I have for you, declares the Lord, plans to prosper you and not to harm you, plans to give you hope and a future. Then you will call on me and come and pray to me, and I will listen to you. You will seek me and find me when you seek me with all your heart. I will be found by you, declares the Lord."*

This scripture teaches us about the mind of God; what His thoughts were, not just **for** the children of Israel, but for His children today. God thinks about you continuously, and unlike man, He does not forget the things He thinks concerning you. That's major because the word "thought" in Hebrew is an accounting term that means "calculated." God has calculated each moment of our lives, the good or bad, the highs and lows, the negatives as well as the positives. No matter how hard the struggles or how many mishaps in your life, you must realize that they are allowed or designed by God to direct you to your divine purpose. He knows better than you could ever know what your value is.

We know because of Psalms 139:17-18, that God thinks about us often and His thoughts are significant and important. How awesome is it to know that the thoughts God has for you are so numerous that they out number the grains of sand? I started to think about how high man can count, and the highest number I could think of was centillion. I would probably get tired before I could count that high, but the word says His thoughts of us are more than I can count. It should excite you to realize from God's word that not only is God thinking about you, but He has specific thoughts about you which means, He is not simply having random thoughts about His children, He has plans and intentions for your life, for God IS thinking about you!